AF269670

Praying Mantis

by Grace Hansen

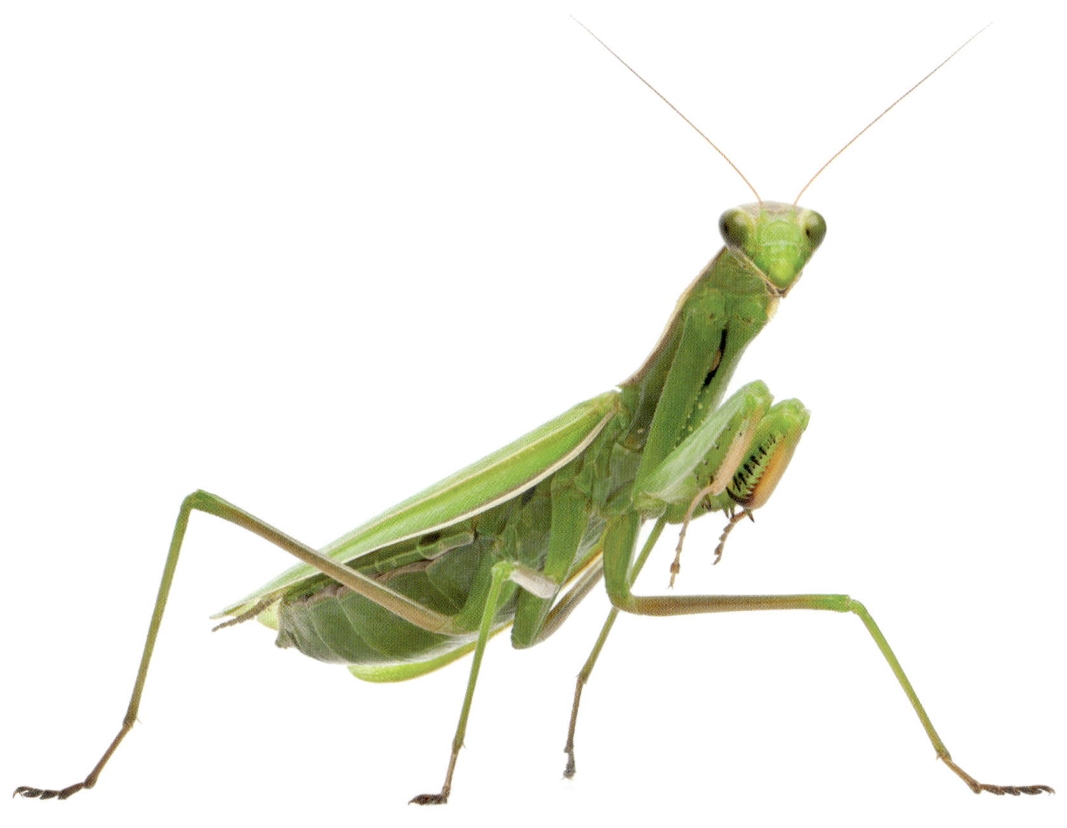

Abdo Kids Jumbo is an Imprint of Abdo Kids
abdobooks.com

abdobooks.com

Published by Abdo Kids, a division of ABDO, P.O. Box 398166, Minneapolis, Minnesota 55439.
Copyright © 2022 by Abdo Consulting Group, Inc. International copyrights reserved in all countries.
No part of this book may be reproduced in any form without written permission from the publisher.
Abdo Kids Jumbo™ is a trademark and logo of Abdo Kids.

Printed in the United States of America, North Mankato, Minnesota.

052021

092021

 THIS BOOK CONTAINS
RECYCLED MATERIALS

Photo Credits: iStock, Science Source, Shutterstock

Production Contributors: Teddy Borth, Jennie Forsberg, Grace Hansen
Design Contributors: Candice Keimig, Victoria Bates

Library of Congress Control Number: 2020947645
Publisher's Cataloging-in-Publication Data

Names: Hansen, Grace, author.

Title: Praying mantis / by Grace Hansen

Description: Minneapolis, Minnesota : Abdo Kids, 2022 | Series: Incredible insects | Includes online
    resources and index.

Identifiers: ISBN 9781098207397 (lib. bdg.) | ISBN 9781644945599 (pbk.) | ISBN 9781098208233
    (ebook) | ISBN 9781098208653 (Read-to-Me ebook)

Subjects: LCSH: Praying mantis--Juvenile literature. | Predatory insects--Juvenile literature. | Insects--
    Juvenile literature. | Insects--Behavior--Juvenile literature.

Classification: DDC 595.7--dc23

Table of Contents

Praying Mantises 4

Hunting and Food 12

Defenses 20

More Facts 22

Glossary 23

Index 24

Abdo Kids Code. 24

Praying Mantises

Praying mantises are a part of a group of insects called mantids. There are more than 1,800 different **species**!

These insects are **native** to warm, tropical places. However, they have been introduced to more areas around the world. This is because they eat **pests** that harm farm crops.

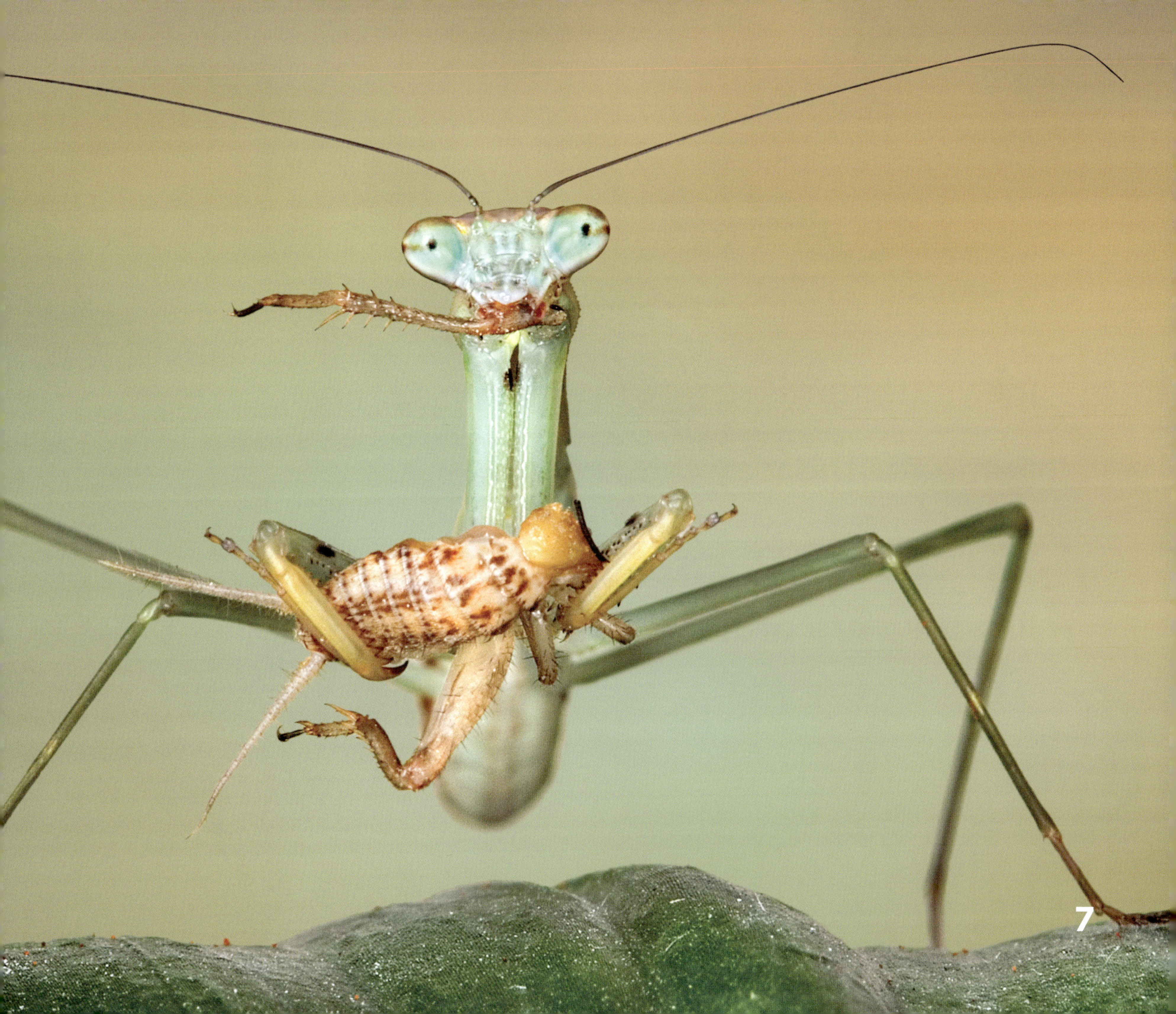

7

Praying mantises got their

name for the way they hold

their long **forelegs**. It looks

like they are praying.

forelegs

Mantises are often green or brown in color. But some **species** are more colorful. The orchid mantis lives in rainforests in Southeast Asia. It is pink and cream in color.

Hunting and Food

Praying mantises look harmless and peaceful. But they are deadly **predators**!

Praying mantises have spines
and hooks on their **forelegs**.
They use these to grab and
hold onto their **prey**.

17

Praying mantises mainly eat other insects. But they have also been known to hunt small reptiles, birds, and mice.

Defenses

Praying mantises can also become prey. But they are good at protecting themselves. They can leap quickly to avoid being eaten. Some species, like the devil's flower mantis, have bright warning colors.

More Facts

- People often call any mantid **species** a "praying mantis." But mantises are actually a part of a smaller group within mantids.

- The Chinese mantis was brought to North America many years ago. It helps keep **pest** populations low.

- The giant stick mantis is one of the largest mantid species. It is **native** to Northern Africa. It can grow up to 7 inches (17.78 cm) long!

Glossary

foreleg – a front leg of an animal.

native – belonging naturally to a place.

pest – a destructive insect or other animal that attacks crops, food, livestock, etc.

predator – an animal that hunts other animals for food.

prey – an animal that is hunted and eaten by other animals.

species – a group of living things that look very much alike, share a similar name, and can have young with one another.

Index

Asia 10

camouflage 14

color 10, 20

devil's flower mantis 20

food 6, 16, 18

forelegs 8, 16

habitat 6, 10

hunting 12, 14, 16, 18

orchid mantis 10

protection 20

species 4, 10, 20

Visit **abdokids.com** to access crafts, games, videos, and more!